# ERic
## SAYS SORRY

WRITTEN BY DAI HANKEY

ILLUSTRATED BY XAVIER BONET

**thegoodbook**
For children

Eric Says Sorry
© Dai Hankey / The Good Book Company 2016

'The Good Book For Children' is an imprint of The Good Book Company Ltd
Tel: 0333 123 0880   International: +44 (0) 208 942 0880   Email: info@thegoodbook.co.uk

UK: www.thegoodbook.co.uk North America: www.thegoodbook.com
Australia: www.thegoodbook.com.au New Zealand: www.thegoodbook.co.nz

Illustrated by Xavier Bonet / Design & Art Direction by André Parker

ISBN: 9781910307526   Printed in India

This book is dedicated to
my four beautifully bonkers kids —
Elen, Josiah, Ezra and Anastasia.

May you grow to know the epic grace
of God in each of your lives!

The sun shone bright on a hot summer's day,
As Eric went out in the garden to play.

He placed the ball on the penalty spot...
Then WHACK!!!!
He unleashed a mighty shot!

Up, up, up sailed the ball above the bar,
    High into the sky over Percy Price's yard.

Thump... thumpety... thump...
Eric's heart beat fast.
Down came the ball with a
thunderous CRASH!!!

"Oh... my... days!" Eric cried in distress,
  As he peeked through the hedge to assess the mess.
A scene of destruction greeted his eyes:
  "Percy's pansies are pulverised!"

Filled with dread, Eric fled to the shed.
Scanning the shelves, he scratched his head.
"Aha!" he exclaimed, "I know what to do!"
And he soon returned with a tube of glue!

He crawled through a hole that he found in the hedge,
  Rolled up his sleeves and took a deep breath...
Then soil-to-pot and petals-to-stem,
  He put the pansies together again.

"Buzzin!" said Eric, feeling quite clever...
That was until a turn in the weather!

A gust of wind toppled the pot,
Which shattered again...
Eric's jaw dropped!

Suddenly a small face snooped through the hedge.
  It was Eric's little sister, who didn't look impressed!
"Oi, Eric, what *did* you do?
  And why are you smothered in petals and glue?"

"I didn't do anything!" Eric replied,
    But little sis knew that her big bro had lied!
Eric was guilty and boy did he know it,
    But if he was sorry, his face didn't show it!

"I'm telling Mum," she threatened her brother.
"Tell me what?!" came the voice of their mother!
And there, through the hole, Mum loomed into view.
"Oh no!" groaned Eric, "Now what do I do?!"

"It was Lillie," said Eric, shifting the blame,
His cheeky cheeks now blushing with shame.
"I'm sure she's sorry... no harm done..."
But Eric could see that he didn't fool Mum!
Eric was busted and boy did he know it,
But if he was sorry, he still didn't show it.

"Don't tell Dad," Eric cried in despair.
"Don't tell me what?!" boomed a voice on the air.
And there through the hedge a third face peered,
And with it all hope of escape disappeared.

"D-D-D-Dad..." stuttered Eric, "W-w-what a surprise!"
But the panic in his eyes could not be disguised.
"Hey, Eric," called Dad, "what's occurring?"
"Eric's a vandal!" said Lillie, stirring!

"Well, it could have been worse..." Eric insisted,
"I didn't smash a window like Lillie once did."
Eric was squirming and twisting and turning,
But his distraction tactic was crashing and burning.

Eric was guilty and boy did he Know it.
    But now he was sorry, and his sad eyes showed it.
"Eric m'boy, we can fix this mess,
    But is there something you need to confess?"

"Yes!" blurted Eric, "It's all my fault.
I unleashed a shot like a thunderbolt.
I've clearly got super soccer powers,
'Cos the ball flew for miles and wrecked these flowers!
So I ran to the shed and raided your shelf,
And I nicked the glue to fix it myself.
Lillie came over, so I told her a lie,
But then I blamed her when Mum swung by.
And now you're here and I feel SO bad...
                I'm really, REALLY sorry, Dad!"

His father smiled and reached out his hand...
"You're forgiven. Now hurry, 'cos Dad's got a plan!"
Quick as a flash Eric dashed back through,
And was met with hugs (despite all the glue).

They cleaned him up and then popped to the shop
 To purchase a pot for Percy's plot.
Eric held up a coin: "It's all I've got!"
 "Don't worry," said Dad, "I've paid for the lot!"

"Thanks," said Eric, "But I don't deserve it!"
   "You're right!" said his dad. "But no one's perfect!
Learn this lesson and never forget it —
   This is called grace — and grace is epic!"

"What's grace?" asked Eric?
"Well," said his dad,
"It's undeserved kindness when we've been bad.
We all mess up, but God loves us still!
Grace puts things right and it pays the bill!"

"Amazing!" said Eric, "But how does he pay?"
"Son," whispered Dad, "there was only one way!
Jesus paid for our sins with his blood on the cross."
"WOW!" exclaimed Eric, "Grace costs a lot!"

"Dad!" declared Eric, "Grace is cool!
  I just hope that Percy thinks so too!"
Eric trudged up the path to Percy's door.
  He Knocked... then waited... then Knocked once more!

The door creaked open and there was Percy.
Eric held up the pot and pleaded for mercy!
"I-I-I smashed your pot and destroyed your pansies —
I'm so sorry, Percy, please forgive me!"

Percy gently took the pot.
"Thank you, Eric, this means a lot!
You've learned your lesson, I can tell.
All is forgiven — I wish you well."

The grateful lad walked home with his dad,
Amazed that grace had made him un-sad!

Eric was loved and boy did he Know it.
His sorry was gone and his big smile showed it!

## A VERSE TO SAY

"But if we confess our sins, he will forgive our sins.
We can trust God. He does what is right. He will make us clean
from all the wrongs we have done."
(1 John 1 v 9, International Children's Bible)

## A GAME TO PLAY

Grace is a free gift we don't deserve. Make a big list of all the
gifts you've been given that you didn't deserve (e.g. an ice cream
when out in the park). Take some time to think about all those
who gave you the gifts and consider why. Finish up by thanking
God for the best free gift he has given you.

## A PRAYER TO PRAY

Dear God,
I'm praying this prayer to say sorry to you,
For all the wrong things I think, say and do.
Forgive me for all of my sinful mistakes,
Thanks for the cross and your beautiful grace.
Amen.